Stars of the Opera 1950–1985 in Photographs

Edited by
James Camner

DOVER PUBLICATIONS, INC.
New York

Published in Canada by General Publishing Company, Ltd., 30 Lesmill Road, Don Mills, Toronto, Ontario.
Published in the United Kingdom by Constable and Company, Ltd.

Stars of the Opera, 1950–1985, in Photographs is a new work, first published by Dover Publications, Inc., in 1986.

Book design by Carol Belanger Grafton.
Manufactured in the United States of America
Dover Publications, Inc., 31 East 2nd Street, Mineola, N.Y. 11501

Library of Congress Cataloging-in-Publication Data

Stars of the opera, 1950–1985, in photographs.

1. Singers—Portraits. 2. Opera—Pictorial works. I. Camner, James.
ML87.S78   1986   782.1'092'2   86-19784
ISBN 0-486-25240-X (pbk.)

Introduction

This volume picks up where *The Great Opera Stars in Historic Photographs: 343 Portraits from the 1850s to the 1940s* (Dover 23575-0) left off. It is a record covering the postwar years to the present.

Although most of the great stars of recent years will be found here, limitations of space and availability of photographs were also factors determining inclusion. With a few important exceptions, duplication of singers represented in the earlier volume has been avoided. We have, for example, included a photograph of Kirsten Flagstad taken in the 1950s because it represents a specific portion of her career that falls within the period we are covering. We have also included images of singers whose careers were of extreme importance to our era, such as Jussi Björling and Leonard Warren. Although some singers are thus duplicated, the photographs of them are not.

Despite the common complaint that there are no great singers today, we certainly had no trouble filling a whole book with the stars of the past four decades. Nor is there any want of glamour with the likes of Sutherland, Norman, Sills, Nilsson, Pavarotti, Price, Te Kanawa, Corelli and Callas. Many of these singers are captured in unusual photographs that are published here for the first time.

The era covered in this book differs from that covered by the first in many respects. The world of opera changed greatly during World War II. Many great opera houses, such as La Scala and the Vienna State Opera, had been destroyed and had to be rebuilt. Later, the old Met was demolished and replaced by the new theater in Lincoln Center.

Traditions changed as well: We see the rise of a new breed of singer, artists who share a versatility and musicianship that allow them to perform in many styles and traditions with equal ease. On the other hand, there are few singers here who have created important roles in world premieres. Perhaps it is the dearth of new works that allows many singers to concentrate on a wider standard repertory.

We also see new life given to the repertory. Bel canto, reborn with Callas, is performed today by such singers as Sutherland and Caballé. There is an increasing number of revivals of Baroque works—operas by Monteverdi, Rameau and Handel have joined the repertory. These changes in vocal technique, performance practice and repertory have set the pattern for the remainder of the century. Through them we can imagine in which works and styles the singers in a sequel to this volume will perform.

Thanks are due Robert Tuggle, Bismark Reine and Richard Arsenty for their generous advice and help.

The captions, although brief, try to convey the salient facts of an artist's career and provide as much data (such as year of birth) as was available.

Stars of the Opera 1950–1985 in Photographs

1

1. **Theo Adam** (born 1926), German bass, as Hans Sachs in *Die Meistersinger*. Since 1957 he has starred at the Berlin State Opera. 2. **John Alexander** (born 1935), American tenor, as Kodanda in Gian Carlo Menotti's *The Last Savage*. Since his debut in 1961 he has been a leading tenor at the Met.

LUIGI ALVA
nel "WERTHER.

3. **Luigi Alva** (born 1927), Peruvian tenor, in the title role of *Werther*. He has been a leading lyric tenor from the time of his great success at La Scala in 1956. **4. June Anderson,** American soprano, as Olympia in *Les Contes d'Hoffmann*. She enjoyed success in the 1985 Paris Opéra performances of Meyerbeer's *Robert le Diable*, and is noted for numerous recordings of Rossini operas. **5. Marian Anderson** (born 1902), American contralto, as Ulrica in *Un Ballo in Maschera*, her single Met role. Her debut, on January 7, 1955, was an event that opened the Met's doors to black singers. Her legendary career as a concert singer began in 1928. **6. Marian Anderson** in her living room.

7. **Giacomo Aragall** (born 1939), Spanish tenor, as the Duke in *Rigoletto*, the role in which this leading international tenor made his 1968 Met debut. 8. **Martina Arroyo** (born 1937), American soprano, in the title role of *Madama Butterfly*. She was a Metropolitan Opera Auditions winner in 1958. Since 1963, she has been one of the world's leading dramatic sopranos. 9. **Vladimir Atlantov** (born 1939), Russian tenor. He joined the Kirov as a leading tenor in 1963 and the Bolshoi in 1967. He has also sung baritone roles. 10. **Arleen Augér** (born 1939), American soprano. A coloratura soprano specializing in Mozart roles, she has based her activities in Vienna, where she made her debut as the Queen of the Night.

11. Gabriel Bacquier (born 1924), French baritone, as Coppélius in *Les Contes d'Hoffmann*. A leading baritone at the Paris Opéra since 1958, he made his Met debut in 1964. His versatility as a singer and gifted actor has enabled him to sing a wide range of roles. **12. Norman Bailey** (born 1933), English baritone. A specialist in Wagnerian roles, he became a fixture at the English National Opera and at Covent Garden in the 1970s. **13. Dame Janet Baker** (born 1933), English mezzo-soprano, is a renowned singer who, until recently, divided her time between concert and opera. She made her Covent Garden debut in 1966.

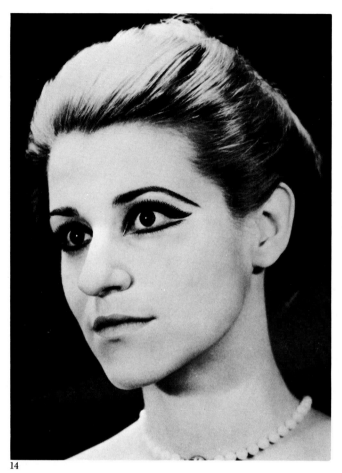

14

15

14. **Agnes Baltsa** (born 1944), Greek mezzo-soprano. A star at the Vienna State Opera since 1972, she has become a noted portrayer of Carmen. **15. Ettore Bastianini** (1922–1967), Italian baritone, as Marcello in *La Bohème*. Beginning his career as a bass (Colline, Ravenna, 1945), he was established as one of the world's leading baritones by his 1953 Met debut as Germont in *La Traviata*. **16. Kathleen Battle** (born 1948), American soprano. Making her Met debut in 1977, she is famous for her Mozart roles, including Despina and Blondchen. **17. Hildegard Behrens** (born 1946), German soprano, as Marie in *Wozzeck*. Her appearances at Salzburg, Vienna, Munich, Bayreuth and the Met have established her as one of the leading exponents of dramatic-soprano roles in the German repertoire.

16

17

18. Gabriella Beňačková (born 1942), Czech soprano, in the title role of Janáček's *Jenůfa*. The leading Czech soprano, she sang Smetana's *Libuse* at the reopening of the Prague National Theater in 1983 and in its American premiere at Carnegie Hall in 1986, in which she enjoyed tremendous success. **19. Teresa Berganza** (born 1935), Spanish mezzo-soprano. Since her debut at Aix-en-Provence in 1957, she has been one of the world's star mezzo-sopranos, especially valued in the florid Rossini operas and the interpretation of Spanish songs. **20. Carlo Bergonzi** (born 1924), Italian tenor, as Des Grieux in *Manon Lescaut*. He began as a baritone in 1948, but changed to tenor in 1951. His aristocratic style and smooth voice have made him one of the major tenors of the day. He made his Met debut in 1956. **21. Bianca Berini** (born 1940), Italian mezzo-soprano, as Eboli in *Don Carlo*. A mezzo-soprano famous for her Verdi roles, she has sung at the world's major opera houses.

20

21

22

23

22. Mario Berini, Russian-born American tenor, was a frequent performer at the New York City Opera in the 1950s. He also sang briefly at the Met. **23. Walter Berry** (born 1929), Austrian bass-baritone, as Barak in *Die Frau ohne Schatten*. He has been popular in Mozart and Strauss roles at leading festivals and opera houses including the Met, Salzburg, the Vienna State Opera and Covent Garden. **24. Jussi Björling** (1911–1960), Swedish tenor, in the title role of *Don Carlo*. He is considered one of the greatest tenors of the century for the purity of his voice and refinement of his musicianship.

25

25. Judith Blegen (born 1941), American soprano, as Sophie in *Der Rosenkavalier*. A leading soprano who made her Met debut in 1970, she is highly regarded for her spirited interpretations of such roles as Adina in *L'Elisir d'Amore* and Susanna in *Le Nozze di Figaro*.

26. Kurt Böhme (born 1908), German bass, as Hagen in *Götterdämmerung*. He enjoyed a long career as a leading bass beginning with his 1929 debut as Caspar in *Der Freischütz*. A specialist in the German repertory, he made his Met debut in 1954.

29

27. Franco Bonisolli (born 1938), Italian tenor. Making his debut in Spoleto in 1961, he established himself as a leading tenor with ability in florid roles. His Met debut was in 1970. **28. Inge Borkh** (born 1917), German soprano, as Sieglinde in *Die Walküre*. A leading dramatic soprano of the 1950s and 1960s in the German repertory, she is also famous for her Turandot and Lady Macbeth. **29. Piero Bottazzo** (born 1934), Italian tenor, has appeared in leading roles internationally since his debut in 1959. **30. Helge Brilioth** (born 1931), Swedish tenor, as Tristan. He began as a baritone, making his debut in Stockholm as Dr. Bartolo in Paisiello's *Il Barbiere di Siviglia*. After further study, he appeared as a tenor in 1965 and established himself as a Wagnerian heldentenor, making his Bayreuth debut as Siegmund in 1969. **31. Sesto Bruscantini** (born 1919), Italian bass-baritone. He has enjoyed a long career as a buffo singer in Mozart and Rossini roles since his debut in 1946. **32. Renato Bruson** (born 1936), Italian baritone, as Ashton in *Lucia di Lammermoor*. Singing since 1961, he established himself as a favorite in Verdi and Donizetti roles during his 1972 La Scala debut season.

30

31

32

17

33. Grace Bumbry (born 1937), American mezzo-soprano/soprano, as Amneris in *Aïda*. Debuts at the Paris Opéra as Amneris in 1960 and at Bayreuth as a sensational Venus in 1961 established her fame. She has sung soprano roles since 1970. Her Met debut was in 1965. **34. Stuart Burrows** (born 1933), Welsh tenor, as Hoffmann in *Les Contes d'Hoffmann*. A suave vocalist who has performed at Covent Garden since 1967, he is a noted Mozart specialist. He made his Met debut in 1971 as Don Ottavio. **35. Montserrat Caballé** (born 1933), Spanish soprano, as Elena in Verdi's *I Vespri Siciliani*. Since her first appearance at Basel in 1956, she has appeared in many roles. Her 1965 Carnegie Hall appearance in a concert performance of Donizetti's *Lucrezia Borgia* established her as one of the leading prima donnas of the day, especially in the Bellini and Donizetti repertory.

36. Maria Callas (1923–1977), American soprano of Greek descent. One of the most famous and controversial singers of the century, her repertory embraced Wagner, Puccini, Verdi, Donizetti and Bellini. She was especially noted for her interpretation of the title role of *Norma*, which was revived all over the world for her. Her debuts included La Scala in 1950, Covent Garden in 1952, and the Met in 1956. Her last opera appearance was in 1965. She appeared with Giuseppe di Stefano in a series of concerts from 1973 to 1974. **37. Maria Callas** as Abigaille in *Nabucco*. **38. Maria Callas** as Norma with Mirto Picchi, Italian tenor (born 1915) (see also No. 66).

37

38

39

40

41

22

39. Renato Capecchi (born 1923), Italian baritone born in Cairo, as Figaro in Rossini's *Il Barbiere di Siviglia*. He has been a leading baritone since 1950, especially in lyric parts. More recently, he has turned to character and buffo parts. **40. Piero Cappuccilli** (born 1929), Italian baritone, as Germont in *La Traviata*. With over 50 roles in his repertory, in the United States he has been closely associated with the Lyric Opera of Chicago. **41. José Carreras** (born 1946), Spanish tenor. One of the star lyric tenors of the 1970s and 1980s, he made his Met debut in 1974. **42. Rosanna Carteri** (born 1930), Italian soprano. Her 1949 debut as Elsa at the Rome Opera established her as one of the most popular Italian sopranos of the 1950s. She has also had a distinguished concert career. **43. Anita Cerquetti** (born 1931), Italian soprano. Her brief but exciting career in the 1950s as a dramatic soprano was curtailed by illness at the end of the decade.

44

44. **Boris Christoff** (born 1918), Bulgarian bass, in the title role of *Boris Godunov*. One of the most renowned dramatic singers since World War II, he achieved great fame as Boris and as King Philip II in *Don Carlo*. **45. Boris Christoff. 46. Franco Corelli** (born 1921), Italian tenor, as Dick Johnson in Puccini's *La Fanciulla del West*. This dashing singer made his debut in Spoleto in 1951. His 1954 La Scala debut established him as one of the leading heroic tenors of the day. His Met debut was in 1961 in *Il Trovatore* (see also No. 199). **47. Fernando Corena** (1916–1984), Swiss bass, as Dr. Bartolo in Rossini's *Il Barbiere di Siviglia*. With his 1953 Met debut, he succeeded Salvatore Baccaloni as the leading basso-buffo of his time.

25

48

49

48. Fiorenza Cossotto (born 1935), Italian mezzo-soprano, as Leonora in Donizetti's *La Favorita*. After her London debut in 1959, she was hailed as the successor to Giulietta Simionato in the line of Italian dramatic mezzo-sopranos. Her Met debut was in 1968. **49. Ileana Cotrubas** (born 1939), Romanian soprano. Her Covent Garden debut in 1971 as Tatyana in *Eugene Onegin* established her as a great favorite. **50. Régine Crespin** (born 1927), French soprano, as Sieglinde in *Die Walküre*. Appearances at Bayreuth in 1958 and Salzburg in 1967 made her one of the leading exponents of German roles. Her Met debut was in 1962.

51

52

53

28

51. Gilda Cruz-Romo (born 1940), Mexican soprano, in the title role of *Aïda*. She has sung leading roles in the Italian repertory since her Met debut in 1970. **52. Phyllis Curtin** (born 1922), American soprano, as Rosalinda in *Die Fledermaus*. Debuting at the New York City Opera in 1953, she created the title role of Floyd's *Susannah* there. She first appeared at Vienna in 1960, and at the Met in 1961. **53. Oscar Czerwenka** (born 1924), Austrian bass, as Baron Ochs in *Der Rosenkavalier*. A leading basso-buffo in German roles since his debut at the Vienna State Opera in 1951. **54. Irene Dalis** (born 1925), American mezzo-soprano, as the Nurse in *Die Frau ohne Schatten*. She has been a leading dramatic mezzo since her 1955 debut at the Berlin State Opera. **55. Suzanne Danco** (born 1911), Belgian soprano. A noted Mozart stylist, her first appearance was as Fiordiligi at Genoa in 1941.

54

55

57

58

56. Lisa Della Casa (born 1919), Swiss soprano, as the Marschallin in *Der Rosenkavalier*. A radiant singer particularly noted in such Strauss roles as Arabella and the Marschallin, she made her Met debut in 1953. **57. Lisa Della Casa. 58. Mario Del Monaco** (1915–1982), Italian tenor. Gifted with a splendid natural voice of great power, he was the reigning dramatic tenor of the 1950s, performing such roles as Otello, Andrea Chenier and Samson. He made his Met debut in 1950.

59

59. Victoria de Los Angeles (born 1923), Spanish soprano, in the title role of *Manon*. An outstanding concert and leading opera soprano, she made her Met debut in 1951. **60. Anton Dermota** (born 1910), Yugoslav tenor, probably as Lenski in *Eugene Onegin*. He became a member of the Vienna State Opera in 1936. Today, he teaches voice in Vienna. **61. Cristina Deutekom** (born 1932), Dutch soprano, as the Queen of the Night in *The Magic Flute*, her most celebrated role, in which she made her 1967 Met debut. **62. Mariella Devia** (born 1948), Italian soprano. She specializes in lyric roles.

63. Justino Díaz (born 1940), American bass, as Antony in Samuel Barber's *Antony and Cleopatra*, the role he created at the opening of the new Met in 1966. He made his Met debut in 1963. **64. Ghena Dimitrova** (born 1940), Bulgarian soprano, as Lady Macbeth in *Macbeth*. A prominent dramatic soprano, she made her opera debut in 1965. **65. Giuseppe Di Stefano** (born 1921), Italian tenor. He enjoyed a spectacular early success as a lyric tenor at his Met debut in 1948. Forays into more dramatic roles were perhaps the cause of the premature end of his career. Between 1973 and 1974, he gave a series of concerts with Maria Callas. **66. Giuseppe Di Stefano** with Maria Callas (see also Nos. 36–38). (Photograph by Christian Steiner.)

68

69

67. Placido Domingo (born 1941), Spanish tenor, as Nemorino in *L'Elisir d'Amore*. The son of zarzuela singers, Domingo made his Met debut in 1968. After becoming one of the world's leading spinto tenors, he has evolved into a major dramatic tenor with an admirable success as Otello. **68. Helen Donath** (born 1940), American soprano. A soubrette in the German tradition, she has been based in Germany and Austria since the 1960s, enjoying success in Mozart, Strauss and Wagner operas. **69. Renée Doria** (born 1921), French soprano, as Olympia in *Les Contes d'Hoffmann*. She made her Paris Opéra debut in 1946 and won fame as a coloratura soprano.

70. Mignon Dunn (born 1932), American mezzo-soprano, as Marina in *Boris Godunov*. She has been featured at the Met since 1958, singing such roles as Amneris, Brangäne and the Nurse in *Die Frau ohne Schatten*. **71. Denise Duval** (born 1921), French soprano. From 1947 to 1965, a leading soprano at the Paris Opéra and Opéra-Comique, where she was noted as a Poulenc singer. She created many roles in his operas including Thérèse in *Les Mamelles de Tirésias*, Blanche in *Les Dialogues des Carmélites* and Elle in *La Voix Humaine*. **72. Otto Edelmann** (born 1917), Austrian bass-baritone, as the Wanderer in *Siegfried*. Making his Met debut in 1954, he was welcomed for his excellence in the German repertory.

70

71

73

73. **Cloë Elmo** (1910–1962), Italian mezzo-soprano, as Zita in Puccini's *Gianni Schicchi*. A noted singer in Italy in the 1930s, she made her Met debut in 1947. 74. **Sir Geraint Evans** (born 1922), Welsh baritone, in the title role of *Falstaff*, in which he made his 1964 Met debut. A versatile singer, he is most famous for his buffo roles, including Figaro, Falstaff, Don Pasquale and Dulcamara. 75. **Eileen Farrell** (born 1920), American soprano, in the title role of Gluck's *Alceste*. A radio and concert singer whose few opera appearances revealed a voice of such size and quality that she recalled Kirsten Flagstad to many opera goers, she made her Met debut in 1960.

74

76

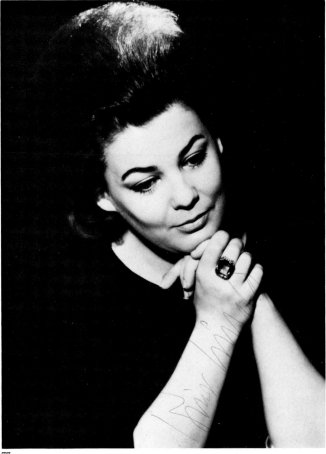

77

76. Kathleen Ferrier (1912–1953), English contralto, as Orfeo in Gluck's *Orfeo ed Euridice*. A beloved concert singer who gave some rare opera performances, including her participation in the world premiere of Britten's *The Rape of Lucretia* at Glyndebourne in 1946. She also gave some memorable performances of *Orfeo*. **77. Birgit Finnilä** (born 1931), Swedish contralto. A concert singer who is one of the few true contraltos before the public today, she has also appeared in opera, performing Erda at Salzburg in 1973. **78. Dietrich Fischer-Dieskau** (born 1925), German baritone, in the title role of *Don Giovanni*. A lieder singer with a large reputation, he has performed in opera all over the world. He has starred at the Berlin State Opera since 1948, and at Vienna and Munich since 1949.

79

80

79. Kirsten Flagstad (1895–1962), Norwegian soprano. One of the most celebrated Wagnerian singers of the century, Flagstad gave some memorable performances of *Alceste* at the Met in the 1950s, and of *Dido and Aeneas* in London. After her retirement in 1954, she participated in the famous first complete recording of *Der Ring des Nibelungen*. **80. Mirella Freni** (born 1935), Italian soprano, as Juliette in Gounod's *Roméo et Juliette*. A leading lyric soprano, she is especially celebrated for her performances in Puccini's operas. She made her Met debut in 1965. **81. Gottlob Frick** (born 1906), German bass, as Gurnemanz in *Parsifal*. He was a classic, dark-voiced bass most famous in the German repertory. **82. Cecilia Gasdia** (born 1960), Italian lyric soprano, in the title role of Verdi's *Luisa Miller*. A sensation at La Scala, Gasdia made her American debut with the Philadelphia Orchestra in a concert performance of Verdi's *Rigoletto* in 1985. **83. Cecilia Gasdia.**

81

82

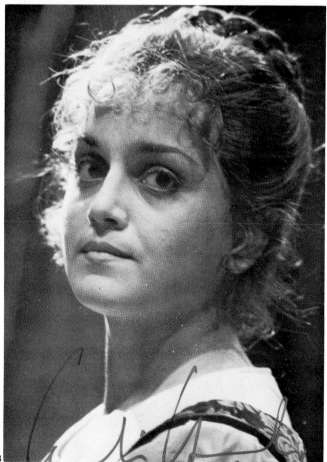

83

45

84

85

84. Nicolai Gedda (born 1925), Swedish tenor, as Lenski in *Eugene Onegin*. One of the most versatile singers of the day, he has starred in lyric and dramatic roles in operas of all national schools and styles. He made his Met debut in 1957. **85. Mechthild Gessendorf,** Austrian soprano, in the title role of Janáček's *Jenůfa*. She has been featured at the Vienna Opera in Wagnerian roles. **86. Nicolai Ghiaurov** (born 1929), Bulgarian bass, as King Philip II in *Don Carlo*. A star bass, he is famous as Méphistophélès, Don Giovanni, King Philip II, Ramfis and Boris Godunov. He made his Met debut in 1965.

87

88

87. Bonaldo Giaiotti (born 1932), Italian bass, as Banquo in *Macbeth*. A smooth-voiced bass, he has appeared at the Met since 1960. **88. Peter Glossop** (born 1928), English baritone, as Count di Luna in *Il Trovatore*. A featured singer at Covent Garden since his debut in 1961, he has also sung at the Met. **89. Rita Gorr** (born 1926), Belgian mezzo-soprano, as Amneris in *Aïda*. A rare dramatic mezzo of the old French school, she joined the Paris Opéra in 1952 and made her Met debut in 1962. **90. Donald Gramm** (1927–1983), American bass, as Dr. Falke in *Die Fledermaus*. A specialist in buffo roles, he also starred in Richard Strauss and Schönberg operas.

89

90

93

94

91. Reri Grist (born 1935), American soprano, as Oscar in *Un Ballo in Maschera*. Gifted with a fine coloratura technique, she has starred in soubrette roles and is especially famous for her outstanding Zerbinetta in *Ariadne auf Naxos*. She made her Met debut in 1966. **92. Edita Gruberová** (born 1946), Czech-born Austrian soprano, as the Queen of the Night in *The Magic Flute*. A leading coloratura soprano, she made her debut in opera at Bratislava in 1968. In 1972, she made her first appearance at the Vienna State Opera. **93. Elisabeth Grümmer** (born 1911), German soprano, as Elsa in *Lohengrin*, her most famous role along with Agathe in *Der Freischütz*. She made her Berlin State Opera debut in 1946. **94. Hilde Gueden** (born 1917), Austrian soprano, as Micaëla in *Carmen*. A lyric soprano of considerable charm, she was ideal in Mozart and Richard Strauss operas as well as in the operettas of Johann Strauss and Lehár. She made her Met debut in 1950.

96

97

95. Margaret Harshaw (born 1912), American soprano, as Brünnhilde in *Die Walküre*. She won the Met auditions as a mezzo in 1942, but established herself as a leading Wagnerian soprano in the early 1950s. **96. Hildegard Hillebrecht** (born 1927), German soprano. She has been a leading lyric-dramatic soprano in German opera houses since her debut at Freiburg in 1951. **97. Jerome Hines** (born 1921), American bass, in the title role of Boito's *Mefistofele*. A popular singer, he made his debut at the Met in 1946.

98. **Grace Hoffman** (born 1925), American contralto, as Eboli in *Don Carlo*. A resident singer of the Stuttgart State Opera since 1955, she has appeared at the Met, Covent Garden, Vienna, Munich and Bayreuth. **99. Elisabeth Höngen** (born 1906), German mezzo-soprano, as Klytämnestra in *Elektra*. A noted singing actress who had a long, successful career of over 20 years at the Vienna State Opera beginning in 1943. **100. Hans Hopf** (born 1916), German tenor, in the title role of *Parsifal*. A Wagner specialist during the 1950s, he made his Met debut in 1952. **101. Marilyn Horne** (born 1929), American mezzo-soprano, as Isabella in *L'Italiana in Algeri*. A virtuoso with a staggering florid technique in the tradition of Marietta Alboni, she is unrivaled in the operas of Rossini and Handel. She made her Met debut in 1970. **102. Marilyn Horne** as Adalgisa in *Norma*. **103. Rita Hunter** (born 1933), English soprano, as Brünnhilde in *Götterdämmerung*. A versatile singer, she has also sung Norma. Coming into prominence in performances of the *Ring* with the English National Opera in the early 1970s, she made her Met debut in 1972.

101

102

103

55

104

105

104. Gundula Janowitz (born 1939), German soprano, as Ilia in *Idomeneo*. A pure-voiced soprano, she has sung at Bayreuth, Salzburg, Vienna and the Met in roles ranging from Donna Anna to Aïda. **105. Siegfried Jerusalem** (born 1940), German tenor. A specialist in the Wagnerian repertory, he has sung in most of the world's major opera houses. **106. Gwyneth Jones** (born 1937), Welsh soprano, in the title role of Cherubini's *Medea*. A dramatic soprano, she has sung Wagner roles at Covent Garden since 1965, and has also performed at Bayreuth, Vienna and the Met. **107. Manfred Jungwirth** (born 1919), Austrian bass, in Lortzing's *Zar und Zimmermann*. Since his 1942 debut, he has sung at major opera houses worldwide, and is particularly noted for his Baron Ochs. **108. Sena Jurinac** (born 1921), Yugoslavian soprano. A renowned Mozart singer who also sang Strauss, Puccini and Verdi roles with considerable success, she began her illustrious career with the Vienna State Opera in 1945.

110

111

109. Raina Kabaivanska (born 1934), Bulgarian soprano, as Queen Elizabeth in *Don Carlo*. She has appeared worldwide and at the Met since 1962. **110. James King** (born 1925), American tenor, as the Emperor in *Die Frau ohne Schatten*. Beginning his career as a baritone, he later became a heldentenor and has enjoyed success in dramatic roles. **111. Dorothy Kirsten** (born 1917), American soprano, in the title role of *Louise*. Discovered by Grace Moore, she essayed a similar repertory of Puccini and Massenet operas. She made her Met debut in 1945.

112. **Sándor Kónya** (born 1923), Hungarian tenor, in the title role of *Lohengrin*, his most famous interpretation. A spinto tenor, he made his Met debut in 1961. 113. **Erika Köth** (born 1927), German soprano. A high soprano excelling in such roles as Zerbinetta and the Queen of the Night, she has starred with the Vienna State Opera and Munich Opera since 1953. 114. **Alfredo Kraus** (born 1927), Spanish tenor, as Nadir in Cherubini's *Ali-Baba*. He is an aristocratic lyric tenor who made his debut as a zarzuela singer in Madrid in 1954, and as an opera singer in Cairo in 1956. One of the world's leading tenors, he made his Met debut in 1966. 115. **Alfredo Kraus** as Alfredo in *La Traviata*.

116. **Evelyn Lear** (born 1928), American soprano, as Lavinia in Levy's *Mourning Becomes Electra,* a role she created at the 1967 world premiere at the Met. Based much of the time in Germany, she has specialized in modern roles and in the two Berg heroines: Lulu and Marie. 117. **Richard Lewis** (born 1914), English tenor, as Troilus in Walton's *Troilus and Cressida,* a role he created in 1954. He has been a performer at Covent Garden and Glyndebourne, where he made his debut in 1947. 118. **Catarina Ligendza** (born 1937), Swedish soprano. She has been a leading Wagnerian soprano at Bayreuth and Salzburg since the 1960s. 119. **Berit Lindholm** (born 1934), Swedish soprano. A leading Wagnerian soprano, she made her debut in Stockholm in 1963, the year in which she also first sang at Bayreuth.

118

119

120

122

120. Pavel Lisitsyan (born 1911), Russian baritone, as Amonasro in *Aïda*. This outstanding singer began his career as an actor in 1932, and made his opera debut in 1935. He made his Met debut in 1960. **121. George London** (1920–1985), Canadian bass-baritone, in the title role of *Boris Godunov*. A star at the Met from 1951 to 1967, he attained a high point in his career in 1960, when he became the first non-Russian to sing Boris at the Bolshoi. **122. Pilar Lorengar** (born 1928), Spanish soprano, as Mimi in *La Bohème*. A specialist in Mozart roles, she made her Met debut as Donna Elvira in 1966.

123. Christa Ludwig (born 1924), German mezzo-soprano, as Kundry in *Parsifal*. She has starred at the Vienna State Opera since 1955 and at the Met since 1959. She is also famous as a singer of lieder. **124. Cornell MacNeil** (born 1922), American baritone, in the title role of *Nabucco*. He made debuts at La Scala and the Met in 1959 and created the role of Sorel in the world premiere of Menotti's *The Consul* in 1950. **125. Jean Madeira** (1918–1972), American mezzo-soprano. A famous Carmen in Europe, she made her Met debut in 1948. **126. Adriana Maliponte** (born 1942), Italian soprano, in the title role of *Luisa Miller*. She made her Met debut in 1971.

127. Matteo Manuguerra (born 1924), Tunisian-born French baritone, as Barnaba in *La Gioconda*. He made his Met debut in 1971, having sung at the Paris Opéra since 1966. **128. Eva Marton** (born 1943), Hungarian soprano. Outstanding as Turandot and in the dramatic-soprano repertory, she made her debut in Budapest in 1968. **129. Edith Mathis** (born 1938), Swiss soprano, as Zerlina with Dale Duesing, American baritone, as Masetto, in *Don Giovanni*. A lovely soubrette, Mathis has been popular in Europe since her 1956 debut. **130. James McCracken** (born 1926), American tenor, as Otello, his most famous role. A heroic tenor also outstanding as Samson, Manrico and Florestan, he began at the Met as a comprimario singer in 1953, left to develop his career in Europe, and returned as a star in 1963.

131

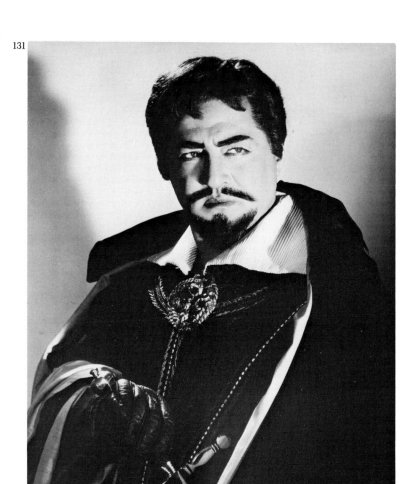

132

131. **Robert Merrill** (born 1919), American baritone, as Count di Luna in *Il Trovatore*. A Toscanini protégé, Merrill made his Met debut in 1945, becoming one of the most popular singers of the day. He has specialized in Verdi roles. 132. **Robert Merrill** with Richard Tucker (1913–1975), American tenor, during one of their popular joint concerts. 133. **Nan Merriman** (born 1920), American mezzo-soprano. A protégée of Toscanini, she had a notable concert and opera career, including a celebrated Dorabella at Aix-en-Provence in 1953. 134. **Mady Mesplé** (born 1931), French soprano. A charming leading soprano at the Paris Opéra and Opéra-Comique since the late 1950s.

133

134

135. Janine Micheau (1914–1976), French soprano. Becoming a star at the Paris Opéra and Opéra-Comique in 1933, she created several roles in Milhaud's operas. **136. Solange Michel** (born 1912), French mezzo-soprano. Making her Paris Opéra debut in 1946, she was a famous Carmen. **137. Aprile Millo** (born 1958), American soprano, made her Met debut in 1984 as Amelia in *Simon Boccanegra*. A rare dramatic soprano, she has enjoyed great success in Verdi roles. **138. Sherrill Milnes** (born 1935), American baritone, as Renato in *Un Ballo in Maschera*. The outstanding Verdi baritone of his day, he made his Met debut in 1965.

139. **Leona Mitchell** (born 1949), American soprano. She has been a leading soprano since her Met debut in 1975. **140. Martha Mödl** (born 1912), German soprano, as Isolde in *Tristan und Isolde*. Beginning her career as a mezzo-soprano in 1945, she began to sing soprano roles, performing Kundry at the first postwar Bayreuth Festival in 1951. She was one of the leading Wagnerian sopranos after Kirsten Flagstad and before Birgit Nilsson. **141. Martha Mödl** as Brünnhilde in *Götterdämmerung*. **142. Anna Moffo** (born 1935), American soprano. Gifted with great personal beauty, she has been a star specializing in coloratura roles since her Met debut in 1959. **143. Kurt Moll** (born 1938), German bass, as Baron Ochs in *Der Rosenkavalier*. Since the 1970s, he has been the outstanding German bass on the international scene. **144. Nicola Moscona** (1907–1975), Greek bass. A Toscanini protégé, he had a distinguished 25-year career at the Met following his 1937 debut. **145. Edda Moser** (born 1941), German soprano. A versatile leading soprano who has sung a wide range of roles, from the Queen of the Night to Salome, at major opera houses.

140

141

74

146

147

148

146. **Carol Neblett** (born 1946), American soprano, as Poppea in *L'Incoronazione di Poppea*, with Alan Titus, American baritone (born 1945). Neblett has been featured at the New York City Opera, where she made her debut in 1969, and at the Met, where she first appeared as Senta in 1979. 147. **Herva Nelli** (born 1923), American soprano. A protégée of Toscanini, she starred in several of his opera broadcasts. Her Met debut was in 1952. 148. **Evgeny Nesterenko** (born 1938), Russian bass. He has been the star Russian bass since his debut in 1963.

149. **Birgit Nilsson** (born 1918), Swedish soprano, in the title role of *Turandot*. The leading dramatic soprano of the day, especially in Wagnerian roles, she made her Met debut in 1959. **150. Birgit Nilsson. 151. Alda Noni** (born 1916), Italian soprano, as Susanna in *Le Nozze di Figaro*. She was a marvelous soubrette who was chosen by Strauss to sing Zerbinetta in the special performance of *Ariadne auf Naxos* given in Vienna in 1944 to mark the composer's eightieth birthday. She was featured at La Scala from 1949 to 1953. **152. Jessye Norman** (born 1945), American soprano. Having made her debut in Berlin in 1969, she has become one of the leading sopranos of the day and is also famous for her interpretations of lieder and French art songs.

153

154

155

156

157

153. **Juan Oncina** (born 1935), Spanish tenor. He specialized in the lyric repertory, starring at Glyndebourne from 1952 to 1961. 154. **Luciano Pavarotti** (born 1935), Italian tenor. A star tenor at the Met since his debut in 1968, he has become widely celebrated as a personality. 155. **Luciano Pavarotti** in an early portrait. 156. **Jan Peerce** (1904–1984), American tenor, as Canio in a television performance of *Pagliacci*. A Toscanini protégé, he went from lead singer at the Radio City Music Hall to star at the Met from 1941 to 1968. 157. **Roberta Peters** (born 1930), American soprano, as Zerlina in *Don Giovanni*. With considerable technical ability in coloratura, she is especially effective in soubrette roles. She made her Met debut in 1950 and sang a celebrated Queen of the Night at Salzburg in 1963.

158. Ivan Petrov (born 1920), Russian bass, in the title role of *Boris Godunov*. A star at the Bolshoi since his debut in 1943, his portrayal of Boris has been compared to Fyodor Chaliapin's. **159. Lucia Popp** (born 1940), Czech soprano, as the Queen of the Night in *The Magic Flute*. A specialist in Mozart soprano roles, Popp has starred at the Vienna State Opera since 1963.

158

160. Hermann Prey (born 1929), German baritone, as Papageno in *The Magic Flute*. The top German baritone since the war, Prey is equally effective in lieder and opera performances. He made his Met debut in 1960. **161. Leontyne Price** (born 1929), American soprano, as Liu in *Turandot*. The leading Verdi soprano of the 1960s and 1970s, Price made her Met debut in 1961. She opened the new Met in 1966, creating Cleopatra in Barber's *Antony and Cleopatra*. **162. Leontyne Price** as Donna Anna in *Don Giovanni*. **163. Leontyne Price.**

163

164. Ruggero Raimondi (born 1941), Italian bass, as Méphistophélès in *Faust*. A fine basso-cantante voice and a good stage presence have made him welcome at the world's leading opera houses. He made his Met debut in 1970. **165. Samuel Ramey** (born 1942), American bass. Incomparable in coloratura roles in Rossini and Meyerbeer operas, he enjoyed a spectacular success at the Paris Opéra in Meyerbeer's *Robert le Diable* in 1985. **166. Nell Rankin** (born 1925), American contralto. She made her debut at La Scala in 1950 and at the Met in 1951. **167. Regina Resnik** (born 1922), American soprano/mezzo-soprano, as Klytämnestra in *Elektra*. Making a successful debut at the Met in 1944 in soprano roles, she reappeared with even more success as a mezzo in 1956. Her versatility has made her famous in such diverse roles as Carmen and Mistress Quickly.

166

86

168. **Jane Rhodes** (born 1929), French soprano, in the title role of
Tosca. A star of the Paris Opéra in the late 1950s, her most famous
performance was as Carmen in the first performance at the
Opéra of the original version with dialogue. 169. **Katia Ricciarelli**
(born 1946), Italian soprano. Gifted with physical beauty as well
as a fine voice, she made an impressive start, winning the RAI
Prize in 1971. She made her La Scala debut in 1973 and is most
effective in Italian lyric roles. 170. **Nicola Rossi-Lemeni** (born
1920), Turkish-born Italian bass, as Méphistophélès in *Faust*. A
protégé of Tullio Serafin (whose daughter he married in 1949),
he was a regular performer at La Scala. 171. **Anneliese Rothenberger** (born 1924), German soprano, as Susanna in *Le Nozze di
Figaro*. A star at the Vienna State Opera since 1957, she has
encompassed many lyric roles in opera and operetta. She made
her Met debut in 1960. 172. **Anneliese Rothenberger** as Pamina in
The Magic Flute with tenor Fritz Wunderlich (see No. 226) as
Tamino.

169

171

172

173

175

173. **Leonie Rysanek** (born 1926), Austrian soprano. She has been a leading soprano with the Vienna State Opera since 1954 and the Met since 1959 in Strauss, Puccini and light Wagner roles. 174. **Elisabeth Schwarzkopf** (born 1915), German soprano whose beauty made her popular as a coloratura in Berlin from 1938 to 1942, and at Vienna from 1942. She later concentrated on the lyric repertory, becoming well known in Mozart and Strauss parts, especially as the Marschallin. She created the role of Anne Trulove in the world premiere of Stravinsky's *The Rake's Progress*. She has also had a successful lieder career, being closely associated with the works of Hugo Wolf. 175. **Graziella Sciutti** (born 1932), Italian soprano. A delicious soubrette, she was especially effective in performances at Milan's Piccola Scala in the 1950s and 1960s. She has become a successful opera director.

92

176

176. Renata Scotto (born 1934), Italian soprano, in the title role of *Madama Butterfly*, her most outstanding interpretation. A leading soprano, she has had a long and sometimes controversial career, and has appeared at the Met since 1965. **177. Irmgard Seefried** (born 1919), German soprano. A leading soprano of great charm, she has been especially successful in Mozart and Strauss roles in Vienna and Salzburg. In the 1960s, she began an extensive concert career. **178. Irmgard Seefried. 179. Mario Sereni** (born 1931), Italian baritone, as Ford in Verdi's *Falstaff*. A warm-voiced leading baritone, he made his Met debut in 1957.

180

181

183

184

180. Cesare Siepi (born 1923), Italian basso. A star at La Scala and the Met since the early 1950s, he inherited the mantle of Ezio Pinza, singing much the same repertory. He triumphed in the Mozart roles of Don Giovanni and Figaro at Salzburg in 1951. **181. Cesare Siepi** as Don Basilio in *Il Barbiere di Siviglia*. **182. Beverly Sills** (born 1929), American soprano, in the title role of *Thaïs*. A well-known leading soprano and musical personality who sang at the New York City Opera beginning in 1955, she achieved success as Cleopatra in the company's famous revival of Handel's *Giulio Cesare* in 1966. Although she had sung with the Met on tour in 1966, she made her house debut in 1975 and retired in 1979 to become director of the New York City Opera. **183. Beverly Sills** in an early candid portrait in San Francisco, in the 1950s. **184. Giulietta Simionato** (born 1910), Italian mezzo-soprano, as Santuzza in *Cavalleria Rusticana*. A remarkable singing actress who succeeded Ebe Stignani as Italy's leading mezzo, she was especially effective in Verdi roles.

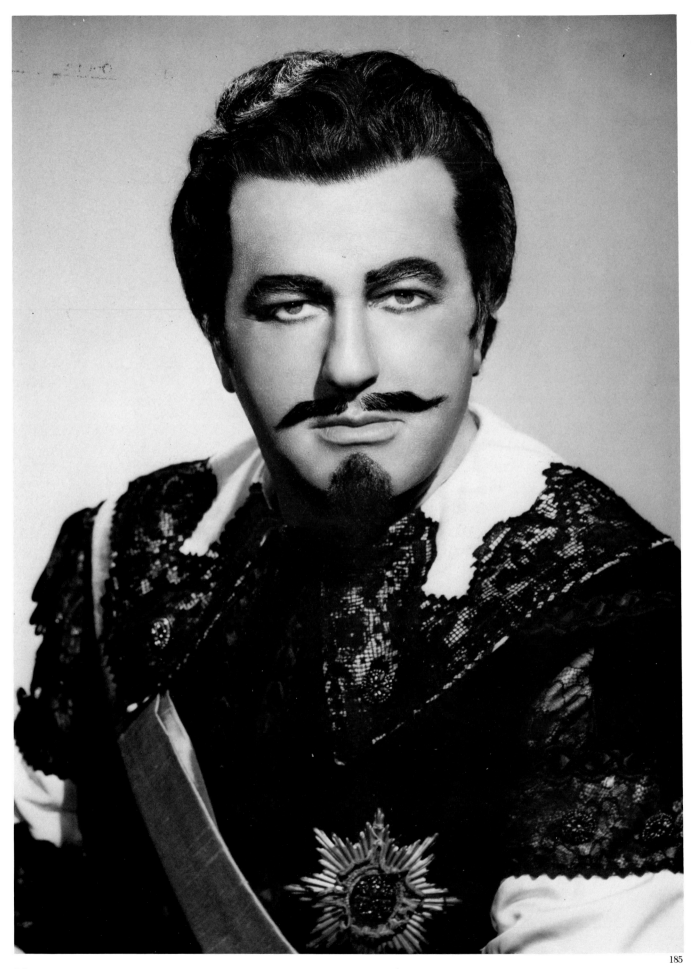

185

186

187

185. **Léopold Simoneau** (born 1918), French-Canadian tenor, as Don Ottavio in *Don Giovanni*. A superb Mozart stylist as well as an authentic lyric tenor in the French tradition, he achieved fame at Aix-en-Provence and Glyndebourne in the 1950s. 186. **Hans Sotin** (born 1939), German bass, as Sarastro in *The Magic Flute*, his most famous role. He made his Met debut as Fafner in *Siegfried* in 1972. 187. **Antonietta Stella** (born 1929), Italian soprano, was highly regarded as a spinto at La Scala, where she made her debut in 1953.

188. Thomas Stewart (born 1928), American baritone, as Golaud in *Pelléas et Mélisande*. He is especially popular in Germany in German dramatic-baritone roles. **189. Teresa Stratas** (born 1938), Canadian soprano, as Cherubino in *Le Nozze di Figaro*. An attractive singer, she has had success in the soubrette repertory. **190. Rita Streich** (born 1920), German soprano. She possessed many of the same qualities as her teacher, Erna Berger, and was prominent in the light coloratura repertory, as well as Mozart roles, in Germany and Berlin in the 1950s and 1960s. **191. Elena Suliotis** (born 1943), Greek soprano, as Abigaille in *Nabucco*, the role in which she made a striking success at La Scala in 1966. She was compared to Maria Callas, but dramatic roles proved too much for her voice and her career came to a fast conclusion.

190

191

192

193

192. Ludwig Suthaus (1906–1971), German tenor, as Tristan in *Tristan und Isolde*. A successful heldentenor in Germany beginning in 1928 and a favorite of Furtwängler, he sang at Berlin from 1941 to 1965. **193. Dame Joan Sutherland** (born 1926), Australian soprano, as Marie in *La Fille du Régiment*. Beginning her career with small roles at Covent Garden in 1952 (including a Clotilde to Callas' Norma), she scored a great success as Lucia there in 1959 and was established as the leading coloratura soprano of the 1960s and 1970s, especially in Bellini and Donizetti operas. She made her Met debut in 1961. She is married to conductor Richard Bonynge, who conducts most of her performances. **194. Joan Sutherland** as Jenifer in Tippett's *The Midsummer Marriage*.

195. Set Svanholm (1904–1964), Swedish tenor. He began as a baritone, then became a fine heldentenor, inheriting many of Lauritz Melchior's Wagner roles at the Met. **196. Ferruccio Tagliavini** (born 1913), Italian tenor, as the Duke in *Rigoletto*. After World War II, he established himself as Beniamino Gigli's successor in the lyric repertory. He made a heralded debut at the Met in 1947. **197. Martti Talvela** (born 1935), Finnish bass, as Fasolt (left) in *Das Rheingold*, with Karl Ridderbusch, German bass (born 1932) as Fafner. Talvela's imposing physical size and voice have made him effective in such roles as Boris and King Philip II. He made his Met debut in 1968.

198. Renata Tebaldi (born 1922), Italian soprano, as Mimi in *La Bohème*. She was discovered by Toscanini, who chose her to sing at the reopening of La Scala in 1946. Becoming the leading postwar Italian prima donna and the chief rival of Callas in dramatic Italian roles, she was unapproached in the spinto repertory in the 1950s and 1960s. She made her Met debut in 1955. **199. Renata Tebaldi** with tenor Franco Corelli, a frequent partner (see No. 46). **200. Dame Kiri Te Kanawa** (born 1944), New Zealand soprano, shown in her native Maori costume. She made her Covent Garden debut in 1970 and quickly established herself as the reigning lyric soprano there, specializing in Mozart and Strauss roles. She made her Met debut in 1974. **201. Kiri Te Kanawa** in an early portrait.

203

204

202. **Jess Thomas** (born 1927), American tenor, as Bacchus in *Ariadne auf Naxos*. Specializing in Wagner and Strauss roles, he sang the Emperor in *Die Frau ohne Schatten* in the opening of the rebuilt National Theater of Munich in 1963. He made his Met debut in the same year and created the role of Caesar in Barber's *Antony and Cleopatra* at the opening of the new Met in 1966. **203. Anna Tomowa-Sintow** (born 1941), Bulgarian soprano, as Elsa in *Lohengrin*. Making her debut in Stara Zagora as Tatyana in *Eugene Onegin*, she has become a leading interpreter of Verdi, Strauss and Mozart roles. **204. Giorgio Tozzi** (born 1923), American bass-baritone. He was a star bass from the time of his Met debut in 1955 and a noted Figaro (*Le Nozze di Figaro*) and Boris.

107

206

207

205. **Norman Treigle** (1927–1975), American bass, in the title role of *Mefistofele*. A marvelous singing actor, he was the star attraction at the New York City Opera from 1953 to 1972 in a wide range of roles from the title role of Handel's *Giulio Cesare* to his remarkable portrayal of Mefistofele. 206. **Tatiana Troyanos** (born 1938), American mezzo-soprano. A leading mezzo with a wide repertory, she sang the title role of Handel's *Ariodante* at the opening of the Kennedy Center in Washington in 1971. She is a noted Octavian, the role in which she made her 1976 Met debut. 207. **Gabriella Tucci** (born 1932), Italian soprano, as Violetta in *La Traviata*. A handsome leading soprano, she starred at La Scala and the Rome Opera in the 1950s and 1960s singing the lyric-dramatic repertory including Tosca, Aïda and Nedda. She made her Met debut in 1960.

208. Claramae Turner (born 1920), American mezzo-soprano. She was chosen by Toscanini for radio broadcast performances including *Un Ballo in Maschera*. She made her Met debut in 1946. **209. Hermann Uhde** (1914–1965), German bass-baritone, as Telramund in *Lohengrin*. He made his debut in Bremen in 1936, was conscripted into the army in 1944 and resumed his career in 1947. A fine singer in many roles, including the Wagnerian repertory and modern operas, he died onstage during a performance of Bentzon's *Faust III* at Copenhagen. **210. Theodor Uppman** (born 1920), American baritone, in the title role of *Billy Budd*, the role he created at the 1951 Covent Garden world premiere. Making his Met debut in 1953, he was particularly esteemed for his Papageno. **211. Cesare Valletti** (born 1922), Italian tenor. A student of Tito Schipa, he was renowned in Rossini, Donizetti and Mozart roles. He starred at the Met from 1953 to 1962.

210

211

212

213

212. Carol Vaness (born 1952), American soprano, made her Met debut in 1984 in Handel's *Rinaldo*. A noted Mozart specialist, she has also appeared at the New York City Opera. **213. Alain Vanzo** (born 1928), French tenor born in Monaco, as Rodolfo in *La Bohème*. Valued for his authentic French style, he made his Paris Opéra debut in 1954. **214. Astrid Varnay** (born 1918), American soprano born in Stockholm, probably as Venus in *Tannhäuser*. She became the leading Wagnerian soprano at the Met after Helen Traubel from 1941 to the 1950s and at Bayreuth from 1951 to 1967. In 1974 she returned to the Met to sing such mezzo roles as Klytämnestra and Herodias. **215. Josephine Veasey** (born 1930), British mezzo-soprano, as Fricka in *Das Rheingold*, the role of her 1968 Met debut. She has been a valued performer at Covent Garden since her 1955 debut.

214

215

216

216. Shirley Verrett (born 1931), American mezzo-soprano, in the title role of *Carmen*, in which she made her 1968 Met debut. After gaining prominence in florid bel canto roles, she developed a wide repertory including soprano roles.

114

217. Jon Vickers (born 1926), Canadian tenor, in the title role of Britten's *Peter Grimes.* One of the most important postwar dramatic tenors in the lighter Wagnerian roles as well as Florestan and Otello, he made his Met debut in 1960.

218. **Galina Vishnevskaya** (born 1926), Russian soprano, in the title role of *Aïda*. She made her debut in Leningrad in 1944 and at the Met in 1961. Benjamin Britten wrote the soprano part of his *War Requiem* with her in mind. She is married to Russian cellist and conductor Mstislav Rostropovich. 219. **Fredericka Von Stade** (born 1945), American mezzo-soprano, as Siébel in *Faust*. A leading soubrette of exceptional charm, she gained fame in Mozart roles and in some Massenet operas. She made her Met debut in 1970. 220. **William Warfield** (born 1920), American bass-baritone, as Joe in the 1951 M.G.M. film of Jerome Kern's *Show Boat*. Famous as a singer in concert, in films and in a few opera performances, he is especially known for Porgy in Gershwin's *Porgy and Bess*, an opera he took on a worldwide tour with a black company. 221. **Leonard Warren** (1911–1960), American baritone. He was the leading Verdi baritone of his day, especially at the Met, where he made his debut in 1938. He died onstage at the Met during a performance of *La Forza del Destino*. 222. **Claire Watson** (1927–1986), American soprano, as a Rhinemaiden in *Das Rheingold*. A versatile leading soprano who was a protégée of Otto Klemperer, she made her artistic home in Germany. She made her debut in Graz in 1951 and sang at all of the major German opera houses as well as at Vienna, Covent Garden, Salzburg, Rome, Milan and San Francisco. 223. **Otto Wiener** (born 1913), Austrian baritone, as Hans Sachs in *Die Meistersinger*. He was a leading baritone in Europe in the 1950s, especially in Wagnerian roles.

220

224

224. Wolfgang Windgassen (1914–1974), German tenor born in Switzerland. He compensated for a light voice by using intelligence to become the leading Wagnerian tenor of the 1950s and 1960s after Set Svanholm. He sang at Bayreuth from 1951 to 1970. **225. Ingvar Wixell** (born 1931), Swedish baritone, in the title role of *Simon Boccanegra*. Famed for his Mozart and Verdi roles, he made his Met debut in 1973. **226. Fritz Wunderlich** (1930–1966), German tenor. At ease in a wide repertory including florid Mozart roles, he was Germany's leading lyric tenor in the 1960s and was considered the probable successor to Jussi Björling as the world's leading tenor until he died in a tragic accident (see also No. 172). **227. Virginia Zeani** (born 1928), Romanian-born Italian soprano, as Cleopatra in Handel's *Giulio Cesare*. A specialist in the bel canto repertory, she made her debut in Bologna in 1948. **228. Teresa Zylis-Gara** (born 1937), Polish soprano. An attractive leading soprano, she has sung in a wide range of roles. She made her Met debut in 1968.

225

226

227

228

119